Beverley Randell

Rhymes About the Bear Family

Baby Bear Goes Fishing	2
Blackberries	4
Mother Bear's Scarf	6
Baby Bear's Hiding Place	8
Baby Bear's Car	10
The Magpie's Nest	12
The New Beds	14
The Toy Train	16

Baby Bear Goes Fishing

"No fish today," said Father Bear.
"The fish are hard to get."
But Baby Bear kept trying,
And he filled his fishing net.

Blackberries

"Yum," said hungry Baby Bear.
"Blackberries are yummy.
Here are lots of blackberries
To go inside my tummy."

Mother Bear's Scarf

Baby Bear went fishing,
And then began to laugh.
The funny fish inside his net
Was Mother Bear's red scarf!

Baby Bear's Hiding Place

Baby Bear was hiding

In a hole up in a tree.

"Boo!" he said to Father Bear.

"Boo! Can you see me?"

Baby Bear's Car

Here's a car for Baby Bear.
He can sit inside,
And work the pedals up and down
To give himself a ride.

The Magpie's Nest

Mother Bear has lost her watch.
Wherever can it be?
It's hidden in a magpie's nest,
High up in a tree.

The New Beds

The beds were standing side by side,

One … two … three.

"Come and see!" said Baby Bear.

"I've found a bed for **me**!"

The Toy Train

Father Bear and Baby Bear

Are playing with a train.

They wind it up — away it goes

Along the rails again.